WINDBLOWN
An Unveiling of the Soul

Poems

Dorothy May

Copyright © Patchwork Press 1998
An Authors' Cooperative
Sharing Knowledge & Experience In Writing,
Editing, Publishing, Self-publishing, Marketing,
& Other Issues Concerning Authors & Publishers
An imprint of Tenacity Press

Edited by
Hal Zina Bennett, Karen M. Daniels, and Susan J. Sparrow
Interior book design by Karen M. Daniels
Cover photo by Susan J. Sparrow

Printed by
Morris Publishing
3212 East Highway 30
Kearney, NE 68847
1-800-650-7888

ISBN 1-892193-00-0

*Dedicated to the movement of spirit
upon the waters of my life*

*And to my human teachers who swim
with me*

THE AUTHOR
Dorothy May
can be contacted at:
1020 Pine Tree Circle North
Buffalo Grove, IL 60089
847-459-1452

Other Books by the author:

Codependency: PowerLoss, SoulLoss
Paulist Press/Whales' Tale Press, 1994

Courageous Journeys
Tenacity Press, 1997

Contents

Part One: Streams of Consciousness

Part Two: Ebbs and Tides

Part Three: Rivers of Silver

Part One
Streams of Consciousness

I.
CARPE DIEM: MOMENTS IN TIME
Poetry on the Now

MOMENTS

Life is created moment by moment.
Moments of fear, anguish and pain.
Moments of pleasure, satisfaction
and joy.
A moment when I'm fully aware
of myself and the beauty
surrounding me.

A moment when I sit at a table
in the candlelight.
The flowers across the table
caress me with their scent.
The scent is red and
pink and yellow.
In the candlelight they softly
glow with their own life.

A moment of remembrance,
when a friend understands,
sees that I'm not always strong,
not always invincible, but
am sometimes needy.

This moment is candlelight.
Scent of flowers.
Wordless in total peace
and silent love.
One of those intimate moments
when time is silent and
all we have is This Moment.
In this precious Moment,
my life has become poetry.
Scenes, metaphors, images,
visions, illusions.
All Moments in the mirage of time.

Fleeting moments outlined
across the canvas of time.
I color these moments with a brush
filled with the paint of
my imagination.
My heart stipples the moments with
with brightness and hue.
My soul sings quietly
as I create my life, in Moments.

What I create is This Moment:
Prayers offered to a god I cannot see
but only hope is there.
Moments of remembrance and of
gratitude for all the
Moments of my life.

Only moments -
remembrances now, today.
Memories are all I have left of
the moments of my life.

THIS DAY

This day shall live
in my memory
when the smell of sickness, decay
and death
is in my nostrils.

I am alone.
Yet am not alone.

I move away from the sound
of artificial music.
The sound of waves, wind,
trees rustling, people laughing.

It is enough for me.

Every thing here is a blend,
every thing a merge,
a marriage.
Every thing but I.

The sky is not empty. Clouds.
An airplane. Sea gulls. Land birds.
I think of him.
And I weep as I walk.

The bluegraywhite of a moving sky.
The windy day.
Warm, strong, vibrant wind
somehow gentle and compassionate.
Like him.

The white sails and bluered cabins
of the boats.
The lake merges its deep blues.
Deeper, aquamarine.

Deep. Still underneath,
lashing and breaking with
the action of the wind.
Just as I.

The graywhite of the gulls,
swooping and lying on the air,
playing with the currents...
as we once did. He and I.

The bluegreenblack of the starling,
cocking his head curiously,
Just as I.

The brown sand, black gravel, greenbrown grass,
occasional objects form a path well trodden.
I do not have to hack one out of the jungle
not today, not this day.

I am alive, even to the awareness
of the insects flitting from flower to flower,
searching for nectar.
Just as I.

A bumblebee, yellowblack, lands
on a clover.
The two become as one.
As one. Not one.
Never one.

And the others.
Just as I.
Then and now.
But never again.

A child. The child has her shirt off
and runs across the grass
to her mother.
They speak motherchildspanish.
Just as I.

Two men lovers,
alone and companionable
on the graywhite rocks.

A man on roller skates
dances by to his own music.
A group of volleyball players
whoop their joy at play.

A pink sweatshirted young woman
and a red sweatshirted young man,
hand in hand,
blown along by the wind.

An older couple, graywhite hair,
moving with the wind.
Comfortable and companionable
with each other.
Not for I.

One older man jumps joyfully
over some boards laid there
for a child's game.
He, just as I, knows
he's still a child.
He grins and points out to
his companion a figure on the lake.
She smiles.

I am alone.
Yet not alone.
I move away from the sound of
artificial music.
This day will live in my memory
forever,
while the smell of sickness, decay
and death
is in my nostrils.

THE HARBOR

My harbor is safe, secure, reliable.
In the harbor my ship has received
acceptance and support and
has known tenderness.

Deep within the ship's hold,
engines are revving up,
making ready to move on.
There is a plaque in the Captain's quarters:
"Ships are safe in the harbor,
but that is not what ships are made for."

So I must sail on.
Alone but not lonely.

My ship is strong and safe.
Fashioned of quality wood and steel.
Forged and welded with the pain
of love given and
loss taken.

The wind that fills its sails is
joy and certain faith
that I must leave this sanctuary
and know the ocean.

TWO DANCERS

Two dancers moving in and out,
in and out.
I turn and there you are.
Another turn and you are gone.

My music moves me
and I am wrapped in cotton.
As I twist and turn toward you,
the cotton blows away...
but I see only ... my own body.

I listen for your voice,
but I hear silence.
I open my eyes to see you
dancing there in silence,
covered by many veils.

A veil is blown away and
for a moment, I seem to glimpse
the beauty within.

But I am bemused now.
And I must dance
to my own music.
Farewell.
Peace be with you.

GOOD BYE AND GOOD BYE

Good bye and good bye and good bye.
To another person and
to another experience.

Fare well. Be well.
I cannot tarry.
I have been warmed by your fire.
I have sat and rested
on your hearth.
I have been refreshed
by your waters.

I leave you with
sorrow in my heart.
I hoped
you would come along.
I cannot go back.

I hope I have
enriched your life.
My way would be much easier
in your city,
but my spirit screams out for
life and living.

My spirit fills my eagle
and flies away.

II.
MASKS OF LOVE
Poems of Lovingness

EROS

See the passionate wave.
Her love is the shore.
The shore at the edge
of the ocean.
He is a warm beach for her.

She fills the shore
with her love.
Then she washes, she swims,
she floats
out to sea.
As she must.

She returns to her shore
when the ocean becomes
too deep, too cold, too wild
for her soul.

The shore meets the ocean
but is not the ocean.
Shore and ocean move and merge,
and boundaries blur.

When the passionate wave
moves out,
shore and water are separate.
But not alone.
They touch.
And are still.
Forever changed.

THE RESPONSE

Fear: A holding back.
An urge, unrequited.
Ability unused.
A dream unrecognized.

A person, half dead.

Awakened now
by inner stirrings -
   of frustration,
   of longing,
for use of Self.

Then:

A hand touched in need.
A shoulder to lean on in weakness.
A response to an unvoiced cry
for recognition of Self.

Heard.

A dream realized.
A debt acknowledged.
Alive at last.
Let be.
Enough.

THE FACES OF LOVE

Love has many faces.
Sometimes it wears the mirror-face
of mother.
Sometimes it laughs and cries
like a small child.

At times when I touch the passion
of love,
it feels like an animal.
Rough and soft all at once,
protecting its own soft belly.
And love is like a rose:
beautiful, perfect, untouchable,
the thorns hidden by its beauty.

Love's beauty lies in the face
of my friend,
sharing the edges of my life.
When I walk around love to see
the other side,
it is Woman, mouth laughing.
Then it is Man, eyes crying.
Another look and it is Androgyny,
standing silent and pensive.
Alone.

For God so loved the world,
that he sent Love to
dwell among us.

Love to comfort us
in the silent darkness of pain.
Love to teach us
in the bubbly laughter of joy.
Love to hold,
to cherish in the infant miracle.
Love to release,
to fly freely with the eagle.
And Love to pull us to earth,
hiding deep within the body.

Love.
It is Elusive.
It is All There Is.

MASKS

Masks. Layers upon layers
upon layers of masks.
A mirror shows me a young-looking crone.
Stubborn, willful, determined.
Group life, community is her task.
Unity of purpose move hand in hand
with unity of self.
I stare at the crone,
knowing there's more to be seen.
Her face dries and crumples and
in its place is woman.
Supportive, flexible, loving.
Appreciative of honesty, warmth
and caring, she merges with others.

Now her face changes shape,
becomes craggy and male.
Analytical, organized and focused,
he holds his own place well.
His thoughts are his own.
He shares them not.

But look! His face softens
and melts down and I see
a young girl, innocent and pure.
She walks with a light step.
Her heart waits for the music
to carry her off to a fairyland of joy.
I watch her face, unlined, soft, expectant;
eyes clear, skin smooth.

Her face becomes oval and featureless,
like a large painting
like a small locket.
And there are layers upon layers upon layers
of faces in that tiny locket.
I close the locket and wait
for another day.

FRIENDSHIP PERFECTED

They were kin: a perfect match, the two.
Children together:
laughing, wondering, exploring,
comparing notes, walking on edges
of lives lived out by others,
incomprehensible to them.

Marion to Ruth is full of color, life, vitality,
A unique creation of her own mind.
Ruthie to Marion is mind, connection,
grace and beauty.
A perfect match, the two.

Young marrieds they were:
building and laughing their way
through the turnings of their young.
Some dark and dreary days shared with
love and acceptance,
each of the other.

Always questions and quests.
What is art?   Why is war?
How is a story? And   Who are we?

Marion sees the movies in Ruthie's mind
and with her gift of sight and graphic words,
makes clear the connections.
Ruthie holds the torch high
so that Marion can see.
A perfect match, the two.

In the last few years:
A commitment made; a bargain kept,
beyond separate lives and private pain.
Deeper than love, broader than blood.
A karmetic connection.
Spiritual, yet rooted deep in daily life.

Eyes that see with clarity,
Hearts that speak with truth.
A perfect match, the two.

A bonding: connection without possession.
Steadiness, compassion without pity.
A closed door open to this friend.
A body enclosed in a room.
A mind that ranges over the wide territory
of human affairs ...
with Laughter,   Wryness,
Truth,   Irony.
Marion connects threads of Ruthie's life
in ways too deep for words.
Ruthie becomes a window to the world,
wisdom and strength and finally:
a pillar for Marion to hold to.

They were kin:
A perfect match, the two.

III.
Healing Fields
Poetry of Family

A CHILD IS

a yet-to-be-formed combination
of two existing individuals
and their past.
A tiny taste of immortality.
The deepest roots of humanity.
The best of both, the worst of both,
a little of each.
His grandfather, his grandmother;
Her grandfather, her grandmother.
No one you can recognize.

A host of hidden needs.
A bundle of immediate wants.
A sponge-like learner, an avid explorer.
A do-er. a dreamer. A dancer.
Inspiring. Exciting. Exalting.
Exhausting. Exasperating.

Awesome choices.
Frightening responsibility.
An anachronism,
birthed from another generation,
and yet: the *future* of us all.
A savage. A creator. An actor. A reactor.
Beautiful. Ugly. Joyful.. Painful.
Easy laughter. Hard tears.
She leaves you with:
little time for each other,
less time for yourself.
No time for trivialities.

He will reward you with:
A smile,   some tears. A strong body,
a searching mind. A loving soul.
 A sticky kiss, a grimy hug.
The Joy of watching the epigenesis
of humanity emerge...
    at its own rate,   in its own style,
    following its own needs,
from a tiny, unformed blot of matter
into a thinking, feeling, unique person
who will give back to life
the gifts received..
IN HER OWN WAY.
      IN HIS OWN TIME.

     L'CHAIM   MUZELTOV

THE CIRCLE OF LIFE

A tiny seed descends and earth is the love-borne;
The seed begins to grow and man begins his song.
The little seed absorbs, instinctively,
and blossoms to a flower, joyfully.

Joyous and awesome are roots in the land;
grateful am I for the nurturing hand.
Even though I choose my growth and my creed,
mindful am I of the birth of the seed.

We are each but a limb of life's larger tree,
for the forest of man is still you and me,
and the circle of love is our manna sent,
while the circle of life is our monument.

TO NAME A CHILD

Welcome, little child,
little girl-child,
with rose-bud lips and
blueberry eyes, ever-searching.

Welcome, little girl,
come learn your heritage,
so you may enter community
with God and with man.

Your name shall be a special gift
to you, to us, to our family.
You take your place among
women, here with us.

You will not be unnamed.
We will treasure and cherish
your name
as we treasure and cherish you.

MOTHER LOVE

I see my child go forth,
stumbling on his pink
baby legs.
I hear him fall and
I can do nothing.
I see my child go forth.
A little herd of children
greet him. I feel them gauge him
and I can do nothing.

I see my child go forth,
into the sea of knowledge.
I watch his victory
blend with his defeat
and I can do nothing.

I teach my child:
love thy neighbor,
that as is done to one of us,
it is done to all of us.
Yet it is hatred
and bigotry that he meets
in his world.

I teach my child:
do not kill,
that if he kills,
he will be killed,
Yet he alone chooses
his destruction.

I touch my child's face.
My fingers caress his hair.
I feel his tears mingle
with his laughter.
But the tears that I taste
are my own.
I see my child's happiness
mirrored in my eyes.
I see the pain of his doubt
reflected there.
But in my mirror, I see me.

I see my child go forth,
the dignity of his soul
stretching forward,
where I cannot follow.
He chooses his pain.
He chooses his growth.
He chooses his joy.

Now my child is no longer
my child but a child
of the world.
And I hold to myself
my joy that I have given forth
a man and my faith
that this man is my most
cherished friend.

MOTHER DAUGHTER MOTHER DAUGHTER

Maiden, Mother, Crone.
so the cycle goes.
The raw edges of our pain
of living in an alien world
binds us close together.

The simple, daily movements
of drawing water from the well,
of feeding our children,
of lighting the fire, draw us near.

An identity: the turn of your head,
a glimpse, a light, a shadow in your eye,
Fingers like his.
Voice like my own Mother.
Yet ...
Spirit free, mind questing.
Spirit of all women.
Soul gentle, taking care not to wound.

Girl, Woman, Sage...cycled once more
at the birth of a daughter.
A daughter-seed, a womb-child,
recognized, birthed and announced.

Oh, womb-child, laid in mother's arms.
Fairy-face, soft as a dove,
nestled in the softness between
head and shoulder, a perfect place.
We pass the torch of womanhood
to you, with the breast of life.

DANIELLE MARIE

The child in pink gingham plays,
toys scattered all about.
Red, yellow, blue spheres,
small sizes to fit a 2-year-old's
tiny palm.

I walk into her safe playground,
green grass and flowers in bloom.
She sees me!
Raises her head in recognition and
with a happy cry,
arms open wide in trusting innocence,
she runs toward me.

Every blonde hair bouncing
with a life of its own.
A tiny angel
whose gossamer wings
only I can see.

Running with the sheer
joy of movement,
of feet upon grass and
wind upon cheek.
Freedom and energy
fly with her.

If I could save one precious moment
and crystallize it
in the glass of time,
If I could reach in and pull out
laughter
to replace the tears in my life,
it would be the moment
when life expresses itself in ecstasy,
shouting, " DeDah! De-Dah!
I love you, Grandma!"

THE SHY CHILD GROWN

Shy is overwhelmed,
big blue eyes staring silently
from the depths of his wordless heart.

Shy is awed, introspective,
full of self-examination.

Finding his own way,
gauging his own readiness,
mastering his own life's lessons.

Unknowing. But caring. Always caring.

Shy is the tentative
soul of a poet:
an imagination rich and clear
but not yet articulated.

Shy is keeping your own counsel
until you are ready to share.
Shy is intuitively honoring yourself
and unallowing others to take
the precious gold that lives
inside of you.

Shy is sorting it all out,
chaff and grain -
for yourself -
in your own way,
in your own time.

My dear child:
Never again fault yourself
for shy.

Shy is a bud not ready to blossom;
Shy protects the rose fully
as thoroughly as does the thorn
on the neighboring flower.

For when shy opens himself,
is ready to show his light
to the world:
the glorious, wondrous, awesome
mystery of a soul in the making
is revealed for all to see
and for all to love.

It is worth the wait.

THE SPIRIT OF FAMILY

A lock of baby-fine hair.
When did those angel faces
become entombed in pain?

An object d'art,
lovingly carried from
a far-away place.

A painting crudely made
by little hands,
presented by
shining faces.

A rock. Just there. The historian.

A small statue of a unicorn with
a guardian angel on its back.
Oh, do angels exist?
Let them exist!

A music box.

A child's hand print in plaster.

Old records. People long dead.
Places no longer important.
Woodstock.

Old ribbons, curled and frayed.
Presents opened and
long since forgotten.

A hand-crocheted dresser scarf
from a time and a skill
long dead.

A pain-filled memory of a time
long ago.
But not so long ago.

A puppet. Fun.

A candy sack. Mmmmm.

A card written in a hand
that can no longer write.

A tiny "Army" jacket.
What do we teach our children?

An old gym shoe,
shaped like the small foot
that once wore it.
Soft and pliable,
vulnerable,
tender and small.

The flood waters wash it all away.

We are moving on.
We are clearing away the old.
We are trying on the new.
We are being with each other
in new ways.

And with the memories,
the treasures,
flow the tears...
a great sea of tears.

And then comes the laughter.
Loud, long, clear
Laughter!

OH, LITTLE GIRL

Oh, little girl,
with your black patent shoes
and white anklets with lace
      all around.
Though I did not hear your infant cry,
nor see your first smile,
      I know your soul.

Oh, little girl
with wide blue eyes
fringed with velvet black.
Eyes so innocent and pure,
      clouded so soon.

Your innocence torn away
like a flower from its stem.
I see you now, so full of love.
Your shattered soul
      searching, seeking, lost.

Meaning comes into your heart,
tripping on soft, doubt-filled toes.
Life beckons you,
      come live with me:
Run through my meadows,
wade through my rivers.
Laugh and love and
      be yourself.

Be good to yourself.
Birth yourself upon my couch.
I fold you, little girl,
into my mother's arms
and kiss your face,
      so soft and pure.
And I birth you into Life,
      that you may breathe.

THE MYSTERY

You bring bits and pieces
 of your life for me to see.
Sorrowful, mysterious, whole stories
for me to hear.
And a wounded spirit
for me to touch.

"It hurts so much; I am under
the pain," you tell me.
Your face and body reflect
fragmentation, terror and out-rage.

You bring me your broken heart
and your shattered dreams.
You let me hold you lightly.
Respectfully, I touch
your spirit.
In you I see the
Child of God's Love.

And then, one day, miracle of Love!
I see a healing emerge
from deep within your soul.
The bits and pieces fall together
and you are a whole being:
And now a Glorious Mystery.

LIGHT THE WINTER LAMP

Light the winter lamp my dear,
for I am home. I am here.
Long these years have I roamed,
I wandered and searched afar.
Far from myself, far from my home,
to follow my star.

Now I return with treasures laden.
I awake, gently aware
of a deep inner rhythm.
A rocking, a cradling.
Never before in my womb
have I awakened thus,

to meet the lighting sky.
A new day, freshly born, pinkly born,
with orange at its creases
and blue at its head.
Velvet black turns to pearl-gray
and peaches, fresh from the tree of life
drop from leafy, lacy branches

Naked trees show their lovely shape.
I, too, am bare bones.
Yet - I am home to light the Winter Lamp.

IV.
The Color of Rain:
Poems of Nature

ICE STORM

The world is awesome
in its cold beauty.
It is as though all rhythm
in nature has stopped.
A drop of rain freezes
as it falls to its own
tiny death.

A small blade of gray-green
grass is transfixed in time,
stiffly standing the same as
when it was captured
by the drop of rain.

A tree bare of leaves,
on which a tiny twig is
petrified, each nodule
to remain forever as when
the fatal drop of water
touched upon and froze
around it.

An indestructible pine,
ever alive in winter's
cold bleakness has felt
the force of the storm.
Its branches droop heavily,
immobile, laden with their
burden of ice.

Yet even now,
buried deep in the earth,
untouched by icy blasts,
the quiet seeds of life
work in silent darkness,
awaiting the rhythm of time
to speak out to them so they
may emerge from their
growing places,
and time will begin again.

And I. I, too, am encased
in ice, my own tiny
suspension. I am entrapped
by the waters of life.

Yet even now, deep within
the core of me, the life forces
silently work toward the day
when my growth has completed
yet another cycle,
and I will once more be free
to follow the rhythm of time.

THE PEAK

I notice the fear first.
Clutching, grabbing,
biting at my gut.
Dear God, let me be safe.

Up the sharp, hard rocks,
over the side a sheer drop.
My feet feel leaden,
my ears ring with the altitude.
Everything seems unreal.
This is too difficult, I think.
There's no way back now.
Too tired... ... ...
can't go any farther. Too tired.
I pull myself up over the last rock,
and blessed heaven!
A plateau appears!
Tough mountain grass, forever brown.
Wild flowers frolic across the meadow.
Colorful scents rise from the ground.

I lie down, breath coming in spurts.
I know now why pilgrims give thanks.
The wind. Oh, the wind.
An eerie wind.
The strongest, most constant wind
that has ever blown through me.
All powerful. God's breath.

Ears roaring, I let wind, sun, altitude
and color carry me to another space.
Turning around to each of the
four directions in an ancient pattern
of blessing, I know it all. I know it all.
The place, the space, the mountains,
move deep inside of me.
North, South, East, West.
I spin like a weather vane,
full of power and life.

Fear dies this day
and courage is born.

MOMENT OF INTIMACY

It was a time of great loss and
of even greater freedom.

The Rocky mountains of Colorado.
My fear of heights runs with me
on doubt-filled little feet.
My breath is sucked away
by the altitude and the winds.
The winds blow through me until
I am transparent,
here on the highest ridge
of mountain in my world.

Wrinkled ridge of stone under my feet,
crevice between sheer bone of rock.
Head pulled up mindlessly
to look across the gulf,
startled by an unknown instinct.

Young, many-pronged, he stands still,
stares unmoving into my eyes.
Deep into the well of his eyes I fall,
souls mirrored in the moment of contact.

My heart dances in the
soft light of his heart.
Transported by the most transcendent
LOVE I've ever known in my life,
from anyone on earth, I know.
We speak with our eyes:

Wetly I propel myself
out of the long, dark,
ridged tunnel of birth
to wobble on thin legs.

Month after month
I am suckled,
as furry posts of antlers appear.
My neck thickens, my rump rounds,
my legs grow stump-sturdy.

In my own body, the shaking begins.
Head pounding like hooves
across the forest plain.
Eyes refusing to focus,
filled with blood.
Fear clutching at my stomach
like death is the hunter.

Wordlessly, we speak:
of foraging for food in the frozen winter;
of siring our young and caring for them;
of hiding among the sheltering trees;
of the endless pain of witnessing
the dying and death of kin;

of running freely and safely
in the sunlight;
of drinking at dusk sweet water
from the mountain stream;
of loves we have loved and
of lives we have lived.

ROCK

Home to seal, otter and bear.
Home to snow, sleet and ice.
I have no home.

Waterfalls have marred my face.
I have lived in the center of time.
The veins of Earth give up their gold
and leave me to my fate.

Birthed deep in the womb of Earth,
cradled in the stream-bed,
caressed by the blood of the sea,
I am the carrier of antiquity.

I know well the story of Earth.
Her sun has burned my face.
Sage am I and white my hair,
soft my ancient voice.

Pressed inward, ever inward,
until I scream with pain
and then am birthed once more.
Transformed is my shape.

I speak to you
with every change.
Do not be afraid,
for life will have its way.

THE LAKE

White fluffy clouds know,
sitting crossed-legged
on the perimeter of the water.
... Farther out than I can go.

Small, fluffy marshmallows,
tiny balls bouncing against
the turquoise breast
of Mother Lake.

A few white gulls swoop down,
wings spread into the wind,
searching for their food.
One little gull , sitting
on top of the waves
disappears and bounces up,
sailing a long distance
... I could never go.

... Farther out than I can go.
How, then, can I move through
my own destiny
to reach the unreachable, which
while unreachable, is ever present;
and while unknown, is ever known.

TO TOUCH WOOD

"To touch wood is to touch the
cosmic tree of life."

Walking along a path through
a deep, dark woods,
thick with spongy smells and
sharp brown brambles that have
fallen from the trees above.

I walk, forever it seems,
on the path that has no end.
All I see are trees.
But the trees are barren.
There is no softness here.

There is no way out.
The path winds around more
and ever more trees.
They hide the sun and they
mask the warmth.
I cannot breathe.
I thirst for life.
I hunger for sun.

Ahead I see a family of willows.
Ah! There must be life-giving,
thirst-quenching water near-by.
The willows are bending and
bowing to each other.
They dance in the bright sunlight.

The supple branches entwine with
each other like loving arms.
I move under the willow trees
to learn their dance,
my soft breast against their trunks.

My fingers caress the leaves.
I feel my heart beat
in time with their loving embrace.

Yielding, tender, flexible, my willows.
Warm greens and tans, yellows.
Drinking the water at their feet,
life-giving and soul-saving.
I am forever grateful
for their Grace.

THE EDGE OF TIME

All the days of our lives we chase
beauty and peace.

Time stretches out before us.
Will we never arrive!
Will we - can we -
capture the apex,
the crown of the pastel sunset?
... a fleeting moment in the Western sky
as the sun reflects its own glory,
bouncing off the cloud bodies.

At the edge of the lake.
At the edge of time.
Breathing deeply, I taste the water.
Waves gently fold over the shore,
upper lips blowing out lacy foam.

The door of the sky opens
and I enter softly, reverently.
Narrow roads of pink wind
through blue mountains of clouds.
Mauve slate rock layers itself
and sleeps in the Northern sky.
Eerie orange lights touch
the metal gray of the horizon.

Sweet air bathes my cells in an
ancient rite of purification.
In the silence there is solitude.
An answering stir,
a murmur of my soul.
My insides dance
the dance of eternity,
are coated forever
with magic and color.

To the right, points of candle stars
greet us with their tiny twinkling
eyes of the darker city buildings.

A giant angel-artist has painted the scene
in textures rich and varied.
Mauve shadows, indigo ribbons of pink.
Smoky sky dissolving at its edges.
Now the water turns to silver ice
as the sky melts into it and is home.

The artist shakes his brush.
Mounds of color enveloped
by the falling of the light
become fluorescent.

Darkness gathers the colors
into its arms and
raises its textured feet
in the farewell song of night.

THE HAND OF GOD

... reaches out to draw up the water
and whispers it out across the lake.
God sucks up the blue water
to breathe it out clear and clean.

The black storm clouds
pitch forth their sharp yellow blades
into the early morning sky.
They scud across and under each other
in a mad race for life.

Hundreds of white gulls swarm
over our heads.
"Look up," he shouts.

The skies have opened
and birthed their children.
The Hand of God
has blessed us.

V.
AN ANGLE OF THE SUN
Poetry on Creativity

THE EYE OF THE HURRICANE

I am a scale;
he is a crescendo.
I am a trickle;
he is a torrent.
I am a storm;
he is a hurricane.

I thirst for knowledge;
his throat is parched.
I hunger for peace;
he is starving.
I struggle to freely breathe;
his breath is painful.

I cannot see;
he is blinded by his vision.
I cannot hear;
he is deafened by his trumpet.
I cannot speak;
his voice is as thunder.

I clamor for recognition;
he cries, "be still
        and listen to me!"
I cry, "I am unique!"
He booms, "You are but
part of the whole!"
I protest, "My words are
        my own."
He sneers, "and who are you
        to keep them?"

I whisper, "What goal is mine?"
He answers not ... He needs no goal.

I spar with Life's thorn
and its grayness.
He battles for its crown
and its sunburst.
I whisper, "I wear the cloak
of reason. You are naked."
He roars, "Be still, you fool?"

**I AM THE EYE OF YOUR
HURRICANE!   I AM YOU!**

CONNECTION

I have heard the cry of my soul
for release from the darkness
of invisibility.

The pain of crying alone,
of laughing where no
sound is heard.

The despair of
breathing raggedly,
feeling jagged, shattered, separated.
Alone.

My poetry connects me
to other souls striving
to find Voice, to be heard,
to become seen at last.

HOPE

Fear. Stomach knotting in terror.
A voice made silent by neglect.
An urge, unrequited.
Ability unused.
A dream unrecognized.
A person, half dead.

Awakened now
by inner stirrings
of frustration,
of longing,
for use of Voice.

"You bring something unique
into this room and it is
your own voice."

My voice? I cannot hear the words.
I cannot speak. I am silent.
Self-doubt on silent cat's feet
claws at my heart and clogs my mouth.

"Will you read it again?"
Hope sits next to self-doubt
And I read my work.

I am astounded. I am stunned.
I am heard! My heart fills
with hope   and
I am alive!
I have a Voice!

INVOCATION TO MY HIGHER SELF

When I am tired, you give me energy.
When I am blind, you see clearly what I cannot see.
When I am deaf, your ears are open.
When I am dull, your mind is sharp and precise.
When I falter, you hold me tight.
When I can't find the words, you speak as thunder.
When I am sad, you fill me with joy.

You whisper always of Love.

I thank you and I love you,
my dear One.
YOU ARE ME.

A LOVE AFFAIR

Mind expanding. Mind soaring. Mind floating.
I move quickly upward, outward and yet inward
In all dimensions at once.

I seek my Beloved.
She who has always been with me.

No body. All Light.
I first see the eyes: luminous, steady, loving contact.
All seeing, all knowing, fully accepting.
And then the hands:
raised in flower petals of
receiving and holding.

This being knows who I am,
where I've been and
what I'm trying to do with my life.
With her, I am stretched far beyond
what I now know.

And I see, know and understand her - You.
there is a mutuality here.
A relationship between us.
A bridge of absolute love, safety and dignity.

We each stretch out and expand
to meet the other.

What I write will be heard.
Who I am will be seen.
And I, too, listen and see with
the very depths of my soul.
And I write from my
authentic highest Self.

Part Two
Ebbs and Tides

I.
Inner Self
The Inner Side of Life

AM I MY BROTHER?

I live in my head.
My salvation.
My Private Hell.

Soon I know not
if I've spoken the words
aloud...

or only screamed them
in my head.

I am my brother.
My brother is me.

JUST AS I AM GANDHI,
SO AM I HITLER!

MY INNER CHILD

I love you, my little child
because you are good and pure,
and dance freely, unashamedly
in the soft wind of time.

I love you, my little girlchild,
because you are gentle and tender,
a healer.
And your song is sweet and low.

Keep the memory of my caresses
within your tender heart.
Show yourself to but a few.

The Magic of Childhood is
such that you need never grow up.
My inner part of you remains
soft and tender - forever.

Remember always that:
You are loved.
You have worth.
You are valuable.

And then: Be very, very tough!!!

MY WISE OLD WOMAN

Behold, my wise old woman.
Her voice is clear and sweet.
Her face is calm and watchful.

Her heart overflows with love.
Her soul is her own, while
her spirit belongs to God.

She stands on the edge of a cliff
on a high mountain,
an ocean behind her.
All she surveys and all she feels,
meet and melt in her soul.

She is everyone she meets.
She is a magical part
of the ocean.
She is wind.   She is tree.
She is deeply connected
to her roots in the earth and
to her animal past.

She is a knower.
Her vision is not as keen
as some.
Her ears are not as sharp
as others..
But she is a knower.
She knows and she knows
that she knows.

She is certain of her
place in the world.
She knows her purpose
and lives her dream.

She searches and seeks
for higher planes of knowing.
She looks to the only God
she knows...the God who speaks
with the voice of the Universe,
and the God who speaks with
her own voice.

She is all of creation,
earth and the universe.
She is made of the stars.
She almost remembers when
she was a star,
searching for a home,
seeking to manifest
and to do the work
she was sent to do.

She has been sent as a StarSeed,
a GodSeed.
and will become once more
a StarSeed, a GodSeed,
in another life, another time,
in another space.

She is a leader.
She walks ahead of us.
She walks with us.
She leads us to the
Sacred Waters and even into the
Sacred Fire where we, too, will die -
to become more -
ever more of what we are.

For now, it is enough.

Enough for her to walk the earth
in her familiar and now-beloved body
and to hone, refine and enhance her soul
so her Spirit will be free.

Her earthly soul feels free
but unfinished.
More work needs to be done.
Other writings are to come.
More connections are to be made.
I go to meet like-minded others
once more.
Thank you. I thank you for
speaking to and through me.
I am gifted. I am full of Grace.

THE SACRED PLAYGROUND

My wise old person can be
childish, stubborn and destructive.
She is defiant some of the time.
She lives in her past shadow self and
often refuses to release
attitudes and ways
that no longer are needed.

It may be that I have something
of value to teach her.
I *know* that I have.,
In my historical past as an adult,
I have brought her up to date.
I have let her know that she
has lived: in the 1960's, 1970's,
1980's and now she lives:
       in the 1990's.
The decade of completion.
Close to the millennium of evolutionary
and revolutionary change.

In the year 2000,
I will be 70 years old!
I will be 70 years old, thank God.
What scary ecstasy!.

Yet I have gained only a beginning
of Innate Wisdom.;
I have only glimpsed Sophia:
heard her whisper
in the night to me.

My world is a challenging,
sacred playground in which
I find challenging, awesome
playmates.
Thank you, Great Mystery.

II.
ShadowLife
on the Dark Side of the Moon

WHAT HAPPENED?

I hear the grass grow,
the birds chirp and sing.
I *am* the bird.

I feel the dolphins throat
as they sing to one another.
I *am* the dolphin.

Sweet Mother, save us.

The death bell tolls
Where?   For whom?
It matters not.
It tolls loud and clear
for *all* of us!

I see the blackness on the earth.
Murky mix of diseased seas,
gray blobs that once were animal.
More: frozen wastelands,
formless buried lumps
that once were living, breathing,
feeling beings.
Where did the green plants go?

I feel the growl deep in my throat,
needing to attack.
I see the snarl of my fangs,
wanting to bite, to tear open,
as I've been torn.

I hear the roar in my ears
of blood pounding over
the ravaged land.

I sit on the rim of the earth.
I touch the void.
The void is filled with
sound, with life,
  with *nothing!*
        TOO LATE!!!

MY ESSENTIAL WOUND

My Essential Wound is deep and wide.
Its wonder spans my life and my death.
Limitations of mind and body
pull at me and engulf my senses.

Veils cover essential truths.
All is illusion.

Darkness.   I slide down the black, muddy bank
into the tumultuous waters
of the River of the Dead.
Slip and slide into the cold, deep turmoil,
shivering and shaking.

Deep under I dive,
to plummet endlessly, mindlessly,
to the very bottom
where the she-monsters and
slippery, squiggly, hungry mouths
open wide to devour
my soul.

Down into the cave of my loneliness
I plunge, to the rocky, murky bottom.
The whirlpool sucks my breath.
My terror grows as I find no bottom.

Up I come, lungs bursting,
finding no air in the cave of
my disappointment and pain.

Up and out of the water I sail,
ragged hair molded to my head,
tendrils winding into my mouth
like eyeless, black worms
of the deep.

Deep and wide is the chasm
of my mind and body.
No eyes to see, No ears to hear.
Self tunneled into the canyon wall
like a bullet with no target.

Up and out I fly, arms and legs
snake-like in the
dusky, falling light.
Up and up, changing shape as I
fly to the very top of the white, deadly
mountain - lace is an illusion.

Nothing to hold onto.
Nothing to grab,
Nothing to stop my fall.

Off the cliff again,
the dark, swirling waters of the gorge
beckoning me to its sharp, jagged teeth.
No! I scream, this is only a dream,
a nightmare of un-reality.

Shape changes, becomes bird-like,
strong wings whipping a drum-beat
on the air.

Lying on the air currents,
I glide toward the open field.
And I land.
Quiet.   Still.
Motionless.   I wait.

Music soft and silky.
Colors alive with muted tone,
I rise up and slide thru the veil.
Across the threshold,
to wonder and to Truth.

SHADOWLIFE

On a dark and dreary path
in the heaviness of the
blackest night.
My usual gray companion, Sorrow,
does not walk with me today.
I am utterly alone.

Ahead, a figure appears
through the thick trees.
A hooded, caped figure.
Dread and foreboding fills me
as I near her. I smell her
acrid smell.
I expect the figure of Death,
so familiar to me.

I stop on the path,
frozen in fear.
The cape and the hood
fall away.

A strange light filters through
the murky depths.
I scream with terror when I behold:
the head. Not one but two heads!
What kind of monster is this?
Two heads!

One head is thin.
Long, stringy, gray hair.
The eyes - oh, the eyes!
Dull and lifeless.
These eyes are cunning.
A world of hidden meaning
fills them.

The round mouth smiles and
leans into the other head,
as if she had no strength
of her own.

A gasp escapes my lips as I behold:
the second head!
Eyes alight with intelligence,
hair thick: full of life and vigor.
My eyes travel down to the
middle of her body.
There, in place of her heart,
is a frozen, man-made lake.
Quite beautiful, the lake,
large, symmetrical, white rocks
framing its borders.

I am deeply shocked.
I don't know what to do.
What is this apparition
who stands before me?

Have I gone down into the
first circle of Hell and
with my anger,
dredged this horror up
from the fiery pit?

Have I dived deep into the ocean
and haplessly, in my net of fear,
caught a sea-monster?

Where is my beautiful, diaphanous,
dancing Higher Self?
Anxiously, I peer up at the sky,
but it is too dark to see
more than a flicker of light,
a pin-point in the darkness above.

What to do?
I ask my soul.

I could ignore,
thinking to ignore is to surmount.
I could feed the hungry head,
thinking to feed is to nourish.
I could plug the bloody holes,
thinking the blood will thaw
her heart.

Shock becomes compassion.
I move closer for a better look
at the two pitiful creatures -
or are the two of them but one?

I look into the mirror
of my own heart
and see clearly
what I must do.

I invite the figures to walk with me
 for a while on my path and, lo!
I find the path widens
to make room for all of us.

Soon it is morning.

III.
Transformations
Challenges and Changes

THE SEED

I am the seed.
Who has planted me here,
I do not know.

It is spring.
The ground above me is warm.
I feel the sun,
but my eyes are tightly closed.

My outer casing is
still hard and firm.
The earth is quite far above me.
But also quite far below me.

I am closed now.
When I am ready to sprout,
I will soften and open.
Delicately, quietly, surely.

For...
I am a Gift.
Because I am a Gift,
I am also the Giver.

When I peep up above the ground,
I do not know what
I shall find there.
Maybe someone will step on me
and I will be crushed.
Maybe it will be too early
and too cold,
and I will shrivel and die.

Maybe I won't be able to
get through the ground and
will die,
aborted in my growth.

But I will emerge.

I will emerge.
Small buds will appear.
I will feel the sun.
I will see the sun.
I will absorb the warm rain.

I will give the world
my part of the world
my small but radiant beauty.

Amen.

KISSED BY THE LIGHT

A dark night
raining, cold, deep,
dangerous.

The darkness of fear
covers my soul.
I weep and
bow my head
in silent supplication.

Look! The Light appears!
The Light shines through
the ice-covered trees,
crystallized in time.

We are all magically
transformed by the glowing Light
into diamonds of great beauty and value:
Gold, Silver, Pink

Shapes frozen in time and place.
Even the once-ugly mounds of dirt:
transformed ...
By the flowing Light.

My soul opens its eyes and
sings its song ...
Transformed am I into
Beauty and Color and Light.
Shimmering and Shining
for all to see.

THE DANCE OF THE FIRE

Circle the fire.
Feel the power of the fire.
Dance the dance
of the fire.

I dance away from the heat
of the fire.
The burning-wood smells comfort me.

I am once more a child
of the forest.

I see the flames,
living orange-red flames
in the night.
The snapping, popping sounds fall
upon the hard gray ground
in front of my feet.

Dance the dance of power.

ANIMA AND ANIMUS

Out of the blue water emerges
a naked being,
dancing within the laurel leaves
of her life.
A cycle completes itself this year.

The woman, shoulders and neck
soft and yielding,
covers her nakedness with
thin, multi-colored veils.
She dances freely, unbound.
She dances with no tears.

The man, once a stranger to her,
strong chest and stomach rippling,
thighs creased and feet planted firmly
on the ground.
He enters her wreath of laurels
and takes her hand.

He moves close to her.
The two flow back and forth
back and forth in a dance
of love and joy.

They make love, she and he.
Twirl around,
arms tightly clasped,
bodies entwined,
flowing and flying as they dance
the ancient dance of sensuality and
of sexuality.

Twirling, they sink to the ground
together as one.
As one, they flow through
a hole in the universe into
the spider web of life.

Together they are born.
One.

Joy to the World.
Celebration.
A child is born.
Let earth receive my death.
Let hearts rejoice at birth.

And life and death are one.
And life and death are one.

The blending of all
remains in God.

YOU

I was unaware.
Just moving in my own ordinary reality.
Unaware
that I was missing something.

But you. You have your own season,
your own time , place, world.

One night, dark, comforting,
wonder-fully alive,
You were there. Present.
Alive?
Possibly, with the only aliveness
in any reality.

I sensed your Presence next to me,
in my bed.
I thought it was Don.
Chet?
A man in my future?

No. It was You. Me.
I felt your Presence. I held out my hand.
You grasped my hand.
No, I grasped your hand.
But I forgot.
You do not have a hand.
You have a Presence.
It is enough.
I was comforted, reassured.
Loved, quieted.
I love you.
I thank you.

TIME

Feeling so vulnerable and scared.
Jagged edges of Time.
Never enough.

Aging. For the first time,
not enough. Never enough.

Spinning. I know what I need.
I know what I want.
Mind. Monkey mind.
Won't let me be.
Keeps seeking,
     searching,
          sucking.
Wanting,
     needing...
          a way out!
Freedom.
A way out of the body trap,
The mind's ferris wheel,
The eternal ferris wheel.
Up and down, round and round
Gotta let go!

But I'll fall!
All the way to earth.
Below earth, even.
So what?
Angel hands will hold you up.

ARE YOU SURE ?????

HER

I saw her hands first.
Lying in her lap:
thick, bloodless fingers
moving restlessly,
hard-boned, raw.

She didn't have much of a lap.
Only the outline of skinny legs
under her print dress.
Ugly print, a bit faded,
like her eyes.

I think it was her eyes
that got me the most.
Right in the gut.
Watery, empty, washed out.
Pulled back deep
into her sockets.

My eyes moved down.
I didn't know where to look.
I smelled the foul smell of death
around her.

She spoke. Her mouth a thin, round hole
filled with false teeth,
clattering, and making small, smacking
sounds.

She frightened me.
And my fear turned to terror when
I realized that
I was looking into a mirror!

Part Three
Rivers of Silver

I.
Through the Veil
The Poetry of Death

LISTEN TO THE SONG

The woodsy smell comforts me.
Time has stopped again
and there's that ringing in my ears.

The ringing is a thousand tiny voices,
a murmur with no words.
Listen!
There's a drum beat.
Is it only the blood in my ears?
Can I trust my self?
Can I trust this world?

Listen! One tiny creature,
large fairy wings billowing behind,
a sky-blue dress dipped in silver smoke,
climbs upon a huge boulder.
She will be heard.

The voices strengthen, sound swells.
Is it a village meeting?
It is an unearthly village
its hall out of doors,
the likes of which I've never seen.

A voice sings out,
another plays the flute.
How pure, how sweet the music is.

Now other voices join the music-making.
Is it a choir I hear?
Or only my imaginings?

I hear a voice crying now,
a sad, wailing sort of song.
A song of dying.
A funeral song.

ON THE DEATH OF A MOTHER:
THE DEATH OF A CHILDHOOD

The cold gray slab of granite,
her name etched in stone.
Who was this being who ended
as another piece of matter,
to be returned to the earth
from whence she came?

To me, she was Mother Earth.
It was her womb that
preserved my fragility.
She was my childhood.
In the end, she was my child.

The first instant of my genesis
knew her and only her.
From her breast I sucked in
the milk of life.

She was my sanctuary, my shelter.
She was my nemesis,
my first opponent in the battle of life.
She was the best friend I ever had.

With her death, my childhood dies and
I stand alone on the island of life.

Yet ...
What did she know of me?
or I of her?

What could I know of the
moment of her birth?
Of the childhood fears and dreams
out of which she came?

What could I know of the life
she fought so hard to keep intact,
of the legacy she tried desperately
to pass to her children?

And what is the substance of her legacy?
Is it in the genetic material
of my cells?
Is it in the deep recesses of my psyche?
Is it in the words she left me?
Is it in the mother-child, symbiotic relationship
which I, by turns, desperately needed,
simply tolerated,
fiercely struggled against and
ultimately tore away from
 to stand alone?
As she before me had done;
As after me, my children will do.

A connection, an interaction.
An association, a relationship.
What is the substance of this?

Can I see the vibrancy of its life?
Hear it calling softly to me in the night?
Taste its unique essence?
Touch its earthy texture?
Smell its dead smell?

For in the end,
there is death.
Final.
Irrevocable.
Alone.
The final alienation.

Yet, though her body is lifeless,
she lives on for me.
In me.
An engram of memory, but more.
She lives on, forever connected to
and by the umbilical cord of living things,
fed on and by each other,
Coming from the origin of life,
dancing for a few moments,
to be crystallized in time.

The energy of her spirit
has not died.
It is recycled into
the gestalt of living.

I see her face every day
in my mirror
and in the faces of her loved ones.

Goodbye, Mother.
You loved me well.
We grow not in each other's shadow.

I stand straight and tall.

HIS HANDS LIE STILL

His hands lie still,
the fingers laced loosely together
like old, white yarn
unraveling down to bloodless fingertips,
where there should be white-edged,
lacy pink pearls:
little pink peppermint sticks of tenderness.

"Magic hands, Daddy!"
        "Fluff up our pillows, Dad."

No more! For his hands lie still.
Still - still as his silent laughter
ringing in my ears,
in the hallways of my mind.

"Bananas!" he crows triumphantly. He holds up
a cluster of brown-spotted, yellow cylinders.
"Good for your potassium level,"
he rejoices.

The taste of our tears mingle
with the smell of incense,
of dear Father Pacelli.
The man's a saint,
to pray all night with Don.
That black, bottomless well of a
last night...
the night he left me
forever.

Those hands will never again
take up a tool
to mend a broken toy,
or a battered dream of a child.

The shattered mirror of our lives
and of our love
lies still...
to move no more.

Those hands will never again
smooth a piece of wood
until the grain stands up fresh and new
as the tree from whence he came.
...or tightly stretch a canvas over a frame
for a painting he will never paint.

I look at his face, beautiful
and vulnerable in sleep.
I wonder how love can reach
so deeply
into my very soul,
into the depths of my being.

I listen for the sound of his key
fitting into the lock he so carefully
and lovingly oiled.
Was it just last night?

His footsteps echoing in the smelly, woodsy
hallway of our minds.
The car radio blaring his Wagnarian ride
through the sky, and
heralding his homecoming.

I touch his eyelids, velvety soft and
moist with unshed tears for his loved ones,
himself and his last illness ...
the one that struck from behind
with the reeling force of a volcano
erupting poisons upon the earth
of his dear, strong body.

When did I last feel his manhood?
His wonderful "instrument of mass impregnation"
thrusting like a wounded bird against
my thighs?
Dear God, Was it only last night?

His smile, his dear eyes, so dulled with pain.
All gone, lost, my lost love.
His hands lie still.

"You light up my life,
you give me hope to carry on.
And you fill my life with song."
Alas! The light is gone!

My rock...my anchor.
What will keep me steady now
that his hands lie still?
Immobile like the dead, crooked man
in our children's nursery rhyme.
Still - so still - in the casket of pain,
in front of the altar where we once
were joined.

Now he is one with his God.
He is Home.
Was it only last night?
That he came home, to rest in peace,
in front of the fire of my warmth
and my love?
Warmed by the very wood he loved
so much to carve?

Life, once an adventure,
now seems empty and desolate.
His hands lie still.

THE PARTING

We have met and shared
an important part of life.

We have avoided death.
We have peeked obscurely at death.
We have confronted death in sidelong glances.

Death has been too final,
too isolated
to stay long in our midst,
for he is the part of Life
which comes in sorrow, in mourning and
tears at our insides with
the Pain of Loss.

I feel a loss at our parting.
This parting is for me a small death.

We meet. We share. We part.

What can I give to you
at the moment of our parting?

A tear?
       A joke?
             A tender sigh?

A bit of myself to carry away with you:
as I have a bit of you.

THE DANCE

The music begins
before I arrive.
Yet I have known this music
always.

The veils of the dancers flow
multi-colored and of different tones.
Pinkredorange.   Bluegreenpurple.
Yellowbrowngold. And gray.

I weave in and out
among the dancers.
I move close to one, then away,
moving rhythmically with the mood
of time and place.

A dancer takes my hand
and twirls me around.
I love the movement.
I love the dance.
Arms encircling;
bodies in tune.

Our veils blow away and I
am astounded by the
beauty within.

We touch. We move close.
We are One.
We part to see through and beyond
the veil of the Other.

We dance without our veils for
a timeless moment.
And then,
the music moves us apart
forever.

The Dance continues...
without me.

II.
Soul Soarings
Voices of Soul

SOUL

Does the poplar tree,
beneath whose branches
I first glimpsed my soul,
have a soul of its own?

Does the soul of the maple,
dressing for its own funeral
with brilliant red and yellow,
praise God in its dying?

MY WILLOW

Throughout the changing
seasons of my life,
you are there.

Rooted in solid ground,
you sway with the wind.
I sway with you,
doing the dance
of life and living.

I trust you.

The clouds were there
all the time.
I didn't notice them
until one day.

One day, walking
in meditation,
I looked up.

The sky began to break
into pieces and moisture
began to precipitate
into the separate drops
that we call rain.

> Like you.
> Like me.
> Like God.

THE SOUL ARTIST

I paint my soul with dazzling color.
Across the portholes of time
   my brush flies.

A ribbon of color and movement,
forming and reforming,
  in and out,   up and down,
  up and down,   in and out.
As the waves rush to the shore,
they return to merge with the sea.

I rock with the energy of the life
within my soul and heart.
Rocking, moving, changing,
   like a giant kaleidoscope.

Meaning lives in the pattern of colors
   and the cloud of my mind
   knows no words.

There is, instead, a quiet space,
a deep place filled with
   light and hue.

Lo! A soft whisper I hear.
I perceive the sounds peculiar
to this unplanned place:
   high and low,
   deep and soft.
All sounds merge into one
harmonious rhythm:
   the rhythm of my life.

My heart is filled with
love and gratitude
and my soul sings her song
   softly and clearly,
   here in my unplanned place.

Thank you my soul, for your portrait.

THUS SPEAKS MY SOUL

Soul is the space between thoughts,
the words between space.,
Its only words lie in The Silence.

Soul speaks in our poetry, soaring
through the deepest myths of ourselves.

Soul is sound, shimmering
throughout the universe with its music.
Her song is like choirs of angels.

Soul has no form but exists outside time and space.

Soul is infinity: the deepest of the deep;
the highest of the high.

Soul is she who laughs bawdily in the
highest realms of our imagination.
Soul is color, brightness, hue,
Splashing across our universe.

Soul is the radiance of the sun,
the star that shines within our hearts.

Soul is the shore of God
floating in the Universe,
connected by the silver thread
of Life.

Soul speaks with harmony
in each of our voices, one to another.
Soul can be defined only by
its expressions in the world:

Wild horses pounding across a plain,
driven by an unknown force.
A small boy, face smudged with dirt,
holding a flattened piece of bread
to feed a duck.
Powerful geese wings driving through the air
how do they KNOW?
each one following his own instincts,
yet uniquely one movement.

Soul is a flame of ice,
a wind beneath our feet.
Winged legs in motion
carried on the breath of Spirit.

Soul's voice whispers silently in the
deepest, darkest night of our pain.
Soul is the murky depths of the ocean of despair
when we are torn away from all we love.

Afraid, alienated, alone we float.
Disconnected and discontented.

Yet the seed of awakening was planted
before you were born.

It was lost the first time you entered a trance
and moved in your tortured sleep
to fling a stone at your neighbor.
Or when you hunted another animal
to its death.
It was your own death
you experienced then.

You broke the pact and it shows
in the shining in your eyes,
where it blinds you;
in the roaring in your ears,
where it deafens you.

You disconnected from your soul
each time you betrayed yourself
with silky words of the lie.
You shunned and nearly severed your soul
each time you believed the lies.

Look! There's a bit of your soul,
between the broken promises.
A tiny particle lies on its side,
under the declaration of undying love
and the cruel words of "good-bye.
"I found a better lover."

A piece skulks around the corner,
looking for a confidante
who can be trusted, after
a Loved One told the untellable.

A speck of your soul lies on your face,
where a trusted other hurled
your vulnerable words back at you

Dare you think you can reconnect,
put the puzzle pieces of your soul
back together?

STAND BACK FROM THE WORLD
AND TOUCH YOUR SOUL!

For your soul never left.
Your soul never abandoned you to your fate.

She IS your fate.
She stayed.
She will stay forever.
You need only ...
to call to her.
In your deepest heart,
she awaits your voice.
You need only ...
to listen for her.
In the Silence,
she whispers your name.

Soul waits behind every poem,
each piece of music or work of art
that captures your gaze.
She stands within the shadow
of your sculpture.

She sits under your false self
who tells lies that no one believes.
She lies under your rich robes of ermine,
garnered with the death of a baby.

You feel her presence
in the touch of a human hand
in compassion and love upon your own.
You glimpse her face sideways,
in the mirror of a loved one.

You feel her magic in the mountains,
the oceans and the plains.
Even when the volcano, the hurricane
and the tornado engulf your life,
She is there.

Call to her. She listens.
Look at her. She appears.
Feel her. She reaches out.
Touch her. She is you.
       SHE...IS...YOU.